An opir

WILD
LONDON

Written by
KASSONDRA CLOOS

INFORMATION IS DEAD.
LONG LIVE OPINION.

When we conceived these guidebooks, we feared they would fail. Who needs a guidebook when everything can be googled for free?

But then it occurred to us: that's exactly why you *do* want a guidebook. You want lively, trustworthy opinion combined with great photographs. You don't want endless information from a thousand online bots.

We think you are like us: you care about quality, you care about style, you care about provenance, but you don't have time to waste on long words like 'provenance'. You want to cut to the chase: where's good?

If you were to come and stay on our couch (it's a metaphor btw; we have a guide to hotels), these are the places we'd recommend.

Ann & Martin, co-founders
Hoxton Mini Press

The Parkland Walk (no.49)
Opposite: Richmond Park (no.36)

Bow Creek Ecology Park (no.13)
Opposite: Welsh Harp Open Space (no.40)

THE UNTAMED CITY

Whenever I say that I love London most for its bold red foxes and deep green woods, people wonder whether we're talking about the same city. How could I arrive in this metropolis and see it for the trees?

It's only since I began working on this book that I've understood why this obsession with urban nature seems so *un*natural. Coming from across the pond to one of the world's greenest capitals, I assumed that London had long mastered the art of conservation, tenaciously protecting its verdant spaces from overdevelopment. Not so: as it turns out, nearly every place in this book spent decades – even centuries – as something else entirely before being rewilded.

The London Wetland Centre (no.35), for example, was a defunct Victorian reservoir before it was reimagined in 2000 as an oasis for waterfowl. Rainham Marshes (no.14) was a military training ground, parts of the Lee Navigation were overflowing with toxic sludge and Camley Street Natural Park (no.3), behind King's Cross, was a *literal* coal drop yard.

I was surprised to learn that England's forests are better off today than they were 700 years ago. Trees were felled for fuel and timber at such a rate that woodland cover dropped to just seven per cent by 1350. Parliament passed a series of conservation acts in the 1500s, but by the 1900s, forests had declined further, to five per cent. For perspective, consider that the capital you know today is about seven per cent woodland, and is classified as one of the world's largest urban forests.

In a world with mounting environmental threats, visiting these beautifully rewilded places gives me hope. So many of these havens were conserved or created by passionate communities who fought, campaigned, donated, fundraised and volunteered to protect and restore them to their natural glory. Remember that the next time you visit your favourite park or garden, your support is meaningful and your voice, powerful.

Throughout this book, you may wonder what 'counts' as wild in a country where bears were hunted to extinction over a thousand years ago, where vast swathes of prehistoric farmland remain agricultural and where even much 'ancient' woodland is little more than 400 years old. While you may not find utter 'wilderness' within these pages, you will find muddy, tree-lined paths where you can smell the earth, urban wildlife reserves where nature appears fully in control and dozens of respites that feel far removed from the city – even if you're still technically within it.

So, grab your binoculars and get out there to explore London's best-kept secret: its wonderful, most natural self.

Kassondra Cloos
London, 2026

Kassondra Cloos is a London-based writer originally from New England. She writes about travel and nature for Adventure.com, *Outside* magazine and *The Independent*, among others, and can occasionally be spotted paddling a folding kayak around Hackney.

BEST FOR...

An inner-city oasis

Stepping out of the office for a few breaths among the trees can dramatically boost your mood. For an urban nature fix, amble under the leafy canopy at Camley Street Natural Park (no.3), snag a bench at the Phoenix Garden (no.4) or grab a pint at Dalston Eastern Curve Garden (no.18).

Urban trekking

Hundreds of miles of walking paths criss-cross and encircle London, connecting its glorious green spaces. Trek the historic Thames Path (no.6) from city to source or immerse yourself in a hidden forest corridor on the Parkland Walk (no.49).

The great outdoors – indoors

Desperate for some time outside but looking to weatherproof your excursion? Escape the rain amid tropical plants in the glasshouse at Avery Hill Winter Garden (no.25) or study rare species in the Brutalist Barbican Conservatory (no.2).

Family-friendly adventures

Little ones in tow? Plan a happy day of adventuring at River Lee Country Park (no.64), with land and water pursuits for all ages and abilities. Head to Horsenden Hill (no.37) to seek out *The Gruffalo* in between thrilling playground and farm visits.

Spectacular views

You don't have to scale dizzy heights to lay your eyes on spectacular landscapes in and around the capital. The vista from Terrace Gardens (no.38) is so breathtaking that it's protected by Parliament and the steep hills of the Seven Sisters walk (no.60) are well worth the burn for the clifftop views.

Birdwatching

London is a birdwatcher's paradise, with a diverse array of wetland, woodland and heathland habitats drawing hundreds of species. Head to the London Wetland Centre (no.35) and RSPB Rainham Marshes (no.14) for the best observation hides, and Amwell Nature Reserve (no.59) for its winning combination of stunning views, rare species and solitude.

Wildlife education

There are lots of simple ways you can help the capital become a more welcoming habitat for plants and animals. Learn how to rewild your own patch at the Centre for Wildlife Gardening (no.24), volunteer with the London Wildlife Trust (no.5) or join an educational walk at Walthamstow Wetlands (no.41).

Off-grid weekends

Craving an extended escape to recharge your battery? It's hard to beat a weekend in the woods for a restorative retreat immersed in nature. Architect's Holiday (no.62) is truly engulfed by trees – as is their swoon-worthy sauna – and the dozens of Unplugged (no.61) cabins offer an incredible array of digital detox getaways to choose from.

STAY SAFE,
LEAVE NO TRACE

Stick to the path

Protect yourself and fragile vegetation by keeping to established trails, even if that means trudging through mud. When you forge a new route, you trample fragile vegetation, leaving tracks that others may follow.

Bin it or bring it home

Many of the places in this book don't have facilities or litter bins. If you're planning a picnic, bring a bag for rubbish and be prepared to pack away everything you bring, including leftover food and dog waste. Even biodegradable waste can be harmful to wildlife and ecosystems.

Plan ahead and be prepared

Before you set off, double-check opening hours and carry a torch if there's a chance you might be out after dark. Bring weather-appropriate layers and wear suitable walking shoes to ensure you stay warm and dry – and don't have to end your day early just because of a rain shower.

Leave wild animals be

Unless you're at a city farm where you're invited to meet the animals, never touch or approach wildlife, no matter how cute or cuddly it may appear. Give a wide berth to grazing livestock and don't feed the animals – it could harm their health.

Keep dogs on the lead where required

Even the best-loved and most-trusted pets can find it hard to resist chasing livestock, small birds and animals. Don't bring dogs to places where they're not allowed and always keep them on lead where requested.

Forage wisely and respectfully

Wild berries and herbs can be exciting to find, but only if you're certain they're safe to eat. Check local foraging guidelines thoroughly and make sure you obtain any necessary permits before you start collecting. Take only what you need and leave some for others to enjoy, too.

Use your indoor voices outdoors

The stiller and quieter you can be, the more likely you are to spot elusive birds and animals who spend most of their time hiding underground or in the trees. Particularly in bird hides, keep noise to a minimum out of respect for both the wildlife and your fellow birdwatchers.

Pack a map and know your way out

Mobile signal can be unreliable, and it's easy to get confused about which way is out. Bring a local map with you and take a photo of any maps posted by the entrance gates, as well as key phone numbers for park-related emergencies. Further away from the city centre, have a backup transport plan in case a bus or train gets cancelled.

1

CHRISTCHURCH GREYFRIARS

Peaceful city oasis with abundant wildflowers

This small, tranquil garden, built amid the ruins of a Wren-designed church destroyed in the Blitz, offers a floral escape that's truly hidden in plain sight. This serene spot can be seen as the quieter, less-famous cousin of St Dunstan in the East (no.7). Though the garden is open on two sides to a busy street corner near St Paul's Cathedral, you're unlikely to compete for a seat here or become an unwitting extra for influencer content. Roses climb up wooden pergolas marking the church's original columns, and floral beds of erigeron, geraniums and dozens of other insect- and honeybee-friendly plants represent the former pews. A grassy, tree-shaded courtyard behind the steeple offers a serene spot for quiet reflection.

King Edward Street, EC1A 7BA
Nearest station: St Paul's

2

BARBICAN CONSERVATORY

Indoor garden in a Brutalist icon

From the outside, the Brutalist Barbican building looks unable to support plant life, but step through the glass doors of its Conservatory and you'll discover a whole new meaning to the phrase 'urban jungle'. Vines cascade from walkways and trees appear to sprout straight from the concrete. Don't skip the upper level, where you can get a fantastic view of the rare and exotic plants. Some 1,500 species are here, including coffee plants, date palms and tree ferns. Admission is free but limited, so sign up for the newsletter to snag tickets as soon as they become available. Hungry? Pop by the Barbican Kitchen to sample its ever-changing menu of delicious and reasonably priced lunch specials.

Barbican Centre, Silk Street, EC2Y 8DS
Nearest station: Barbican
barbican.org.uk

3

CAMLEY STREET NATURAL PARK

Petite yet pristine canalside habitat

Just a short walk from King's Cross station alongside the Regent's Canal, this lush, tree-canopied nature reserve feels remarkably calm despite its proximity to one of the city's most bustling transport hubs. Built on an old coal drop yard, the site has been rewilded to create a home for urban animals. Walking paths bend around wetland, woodland and grassland habitats, weaving in such a way that it feels much larger than its mere two acres. You're likely to hear rustling in the reedbeds, so check the board by the entrance to see which critters (such as blackbirds, reed warblers and toads) have been spotted that day. Finish your visit at the on-site Kingfisher Cafe for delicious hot sandwiches, made fresh.

12 Camley Street, N1C 4PW
Nearest station: King's Cross St Pancras

4

THE PHOENIX GARDEN

Compact community garden

Step away from the hordes of Covent Garden and Leicester Square and hide among the shrubbery of the Phoenix Garden. Few places in central London can make you feel as immersed in nature as you do here, in this green sanctuary built atop land filled with World War II rubble. The charity and volunteers that care for the garden practise sustainable techniques with a 'worry-free' approach, allowing the garden to flourish as it wishes. While you're unlikely to be alone in the garden, its benches are surrounded by native wildflowers, tall grasses and walnut, willow, birch and gingko trees, separating the space into sections that feel almost private. Retreat here for a peaceful lunch amid a busy day of museums or meetings.

21 Stacey Street, WC2H 8DG
Nearest stations: Tottenham Court Road, Covent Garden
thephoenixgarden.org

5

LONDON WILDLIFE TRUST

Caring for the capital's nature since 1981

For more than 40 years, the London Wildlife Trust has been a literal force of nature in their efforts to re-green the capital. With the help of hundreds of volunteers – and plenty of space for more – they now manage a growing list of 36 nature reserves citywide. LWT staff and volunteers are responsible for reintroducing wildlife (including beavers and white storks), protecting vital habitats, planting trees and grasses and creating peaceful respites for all manner of city residents – human and animal. Get involved by signing up to help with one of their many projects, become a member or simply submit your wildlife sightings as a citizen scientist. You'll find a list of practical conservation opportunities and free family-friendly events across the city on their website.

Various locations
wildlondon.org.uk

6

THE THAMES PATH

National trail from source to city

Following the river is an incredible way to get a sense of the ever-evolving relationship between humans and nature. The Thames Path starts in the Cotswolds and its meandering 185-mile trail will lead you all the way to Woolwich in south London. You can't choose a bad section, but the path gets wilder – and more naturally beautiful – the further west you are. There are 80 miles of paths through London, served by historic bridges, river boats, rail stations and tunnels throughout (the Greenwich Foot Tunnel, built in 1902, is a particular novelty, though damp). For an exhilarating pint, navigate to the White Cross in Richmond, which floods so frequently with high tide that the pub keeps wellies on hand for guests.

Woolwich to the Cotswolds
tfl.gov.uk/modes/walking/thames-path

7

ST DUNSTAN IN THE EAST

Green escape in reimagined ruins

Hidden down a narrow alley, the ruins of this 12th-century church have been transformed into the walls of a lush, scenic garden – an enchanting escape from the hubbub of the city. Even though its mossy, ivy-covered arches attract sightseers and photographers, the church's remaining structures – including the Wren-designed tower and steeple, which survived the Great Fire of London and the Blitz – command respect and hushed voices. Popular with local office workers at lunchtimes, it's a great place to steal away for a picnic or coffee with a friend. The garden is hauntingly beautiful year-round, and is also home to some unusual plants: though ornamental today, the vitamin C-rich Winter's Bark was once prescribed to ward off scurvy.

St Dunstan's Hill, EC3R 5DD
Nearest stations: Monument, Tower Hill

8

THE GREEN LONDON WAY

Trailblazing urban walking path

Unless you're a serious ultra-marathoner, you likely won't finish this loop around central London in a single day. But don't worry, it's broken into 18 pleasantly manageable sections of less than 15 km each. Although it was one of the country's first long-distance urban walks when it was devised for an eponymous book in 1991, the route makes use of existing nature trails and London's prettiest parks to keep you enveloped by greenery. The walk is fascinating and scenic at any time of year, but particularly beautiful in autumn when the leaves start to turn along the section through Richmond. There's ample public transport throughout, but no signage marking the way, so bring the book or download a GPS track before you set off.

Various routes across London
greenlondonway.com

9

HACKNEY MARSHES

Vast expanse for football and foraging

Known as the spiritual home of Sunday league football, the Hackney Marshes were home to 120 full-size pitches in their 1950s heyday. Today, the site is a must for anyone seeking miles of uninterrupted green space – or a social 5 km run, hosted weekly by Parkrun. But the marshes aren't just a beloved escape from urban life – they're also something of a natural grocery store. In recent years, volunteers have planted an 'edible forest' of hazel, walnut and crab apple trees offering fruit and nuts for local residents to forage. In late summer, bring a carton to walk along the canal towpath, where you'll find plentiful wild blackberries. Just beware of the thorns, which always seem sharpest by the ripest berries.

Homerton Road, E9 5PF
Nearest stations: Hackney Wick, Homerton

10

EPPING FOREST

London's largest ancient woodland

Home to a magnificent 55,000 ancient trees and some of Europe's oldest and rarest plants, Epping is the capital's largest green space. Having survived since the last ice age, there are countless natural treasures to encounter as you explore. Across its sprawling 6,000 acres of grassland, woodland, marshes and ponds, keep your eyes peeled for frogs, deer, rabbits, bats, badgers and 1,500 species of fungi, and your ears perked for Tawny Owls and Great Spotted Woodpeckers. You can also get stuck into nearly every kind of outdoor activity you could wish for, including horse riding, trail running and fishing. Don't rush off – there's no shortage of eateries within striking distance, including the award-winning Mayfield Farm Bakery and cult culinary gem, the Oyster Shack & Seafood Bar, located in the heart of the forest.

Visitor Centre, Paul's Nursery Road, IG10 4AF
Nearest stations: Loughton, Chingford
efht.org.uk

11
HAINAULT FOREST

Glimpse the past in protected woodland

This land was originally part of the Forest of Essex, a sprawling royal hunting ground. Amble amid the magnificent ivy-draped oaks on Hainault's Woodland Trail and it's easy to feel teleported back to the forest's medieval roots. The woodland almost disappeared in 1851 when a staggering 95 per cent of the forest was felled to make way for farmland. The resulting outcry birthed the modern conservation movement, with campaigners lobbying to protect the park for future generations. Today, visit for a gentle ramble along lakeside and wooded trails – just be mindful of ground-nesting skylarks in spring. Visitors of all ages will also enjoy the petting farm, 'Woodhenge' sculpture trail and balance-testing ropes course. Refuel with a rich and spicy masala chai from Global Cafe near the main entrance.

Romford Road, IG7 4QN
Nearest stations: Hainault, Grange Hill
hainaultforest.org

12

TOWER HAMLETS CEMETERY PARK

Untamed nature in Victorian burial ground

One of London's 'Magnificent Seven', a series of Victorian garden cemeteries built to address overcrowding in the capital's churchyards, Tower Hamlets Cemetery held its last burial in 1966. Today, it serves the living differently: as an abundant nature reserve providing a vital respite from the concrete blocks surrounding it. Vines and ferns have been encouraged to grow freely, jumbling rows of headstones with wayward roots. The grounds are a hot spot for foragers these days (permit required), with many coming to gather sloe berries, nettle, dandelion and cow parsley. Join a guided tour with Forage London to make sure you know the difference between prize and poison.

Southern Grove, E3 4PX
Nearest stations: Mile End, Bow Road
fothcp.org

13

BOW CREEK ECOLOGY PARK

Wilderness in a concrete jungle

Flanked by train tracks on one side and tower blocks on the other, the path leading to Bow Creek Ecology Park doesn't offer many promising signs of what lies within its gates. Stride on regardless and you'll soon see why this small, industrial patch of east London is so special. Here, nature has been allowed to reclaim a river bend that was once dominated by an ironworks and, today, it's a welcome oasis in an area of London that's thirsty for pockets of green space. It doesn't take long to walk a horseshoe around the whole site, but if you're a twitcher, settle in. Look out for wading birds such as the red-legged Redshank on the mudflats and, in summer, perk your ears for the boisterous call of a Cetti's Warbler, an elusive bird that's much easier to hear than see.

Bidder Street, E16 4ST
Nearest stations: Canning Town, East India
visitleevalley.org.uk/east-india-dock-bow-creek

14

RSPB RAINHAM MARSHES

Exceptional reserve for dabblers to pro birders

Since being acquired by the RSPB in 2000, this riverside former firing range has been transformed into a huge avian reserve and an incredible habitat for scores of creatures, including water voles, butterflies, lizards, frogs and an astounding array of bird species. Golden Plovers, Dartford Warblers and Lapwings are just a few of the residents and visitors you might spot from four wheelchair-accessible observation hides, including Shooting Butts, which has a fantastic exhibit of artefacts found on site. Bring binoculars or rent them from the visitor centre, which also offers (paid) guided walks and welcomes picnics, as there's no cafe on site. Avid twitchers can rent Purfleet Hide to get exclusive access to parts of the reserve before it opens to the public.

New Tank Hill Road, RM19 1SZ
Nearest station: Purfleet
rspb.org.uk

15

MUDCHUTE PARK & FARM

Bucolic scenes in the shadows of skyscrapers

Mudchute Farm, a 32-acre slice of east London 'countryside', is quite the sight to behold: sheep graze contentedly against a backdrop of industrial steel and glass from the towering buildings of Canary Wharf. Throw on some wellies and take a wander to meet some of the rarest working animals in Europe, including the Tamworth pig, a descendant of the indigenous wild boar. Arrive at feeding time or book a 30-minute 'Animal Experience' to get close to cattle, pigs, poultry, goats and even llamas. If all that fresh air has left you with an appetite, you might wonder if you've *actually* left the city behind when you see the prices at on-site Mudchute Kitchen, serving home-cooked breakfasts and lunches for as little as a fiver.

Pier Street, E14 3HP
Nearest station: Mudchute
mudchute.org

16

HORNCHURCH COUNTRY PARK

Former airfield reclaimed by nature

Just one of many adjacent green spaces in the verdant Ingrebourne Valley, Hornchurch Country Park boasts attractions that will pique the interest of nature and history buffs alike: miles of maze-like rewilded nature trails, a fishing pond and a well-preserved smattering of pillbox bunkers and Tett Turrets from World War II. Nature is still on the rebound here after the site served as a landfill until 1980, but you'd never guess, considering it's home to London's largest freshwater reedbed. Listen for the booming call of the Bittern (and other rare species recorded here) and spot reptiles, butterflies and beetles. For the latest list of sightings, stop by Essex Wildlife Trust's Ingrebourne Nature Discovery Centre, whose cafe feels almost embedded in the reeds.

Squadrons Approach, RM12 6TS
Nearest stations: Elm Park, Hornchurch

17

HACKNEY CITY FARM

Legendary urban farm with wild garden

Tucked away behind a thick canopy of trees, Hackney City Farm is a rural refuge in a sea of boutique shops and bougie cafes. Established in 1984, its aim was to offer young city folk the experience of farming right on their east London doorstep. Pop in to see Anglo-Nubian goats, Pietrain pigs, Kerry Hill sheep, donkeys and flocks of farm fowl, whose eggs you can buy in the shop. Make time to enjoy the plentiful wild garden, with its orchard, vegetable and herb gardens, and for a light bite at the on-site Frizzante Cafe, serving Italian fare. Check the farm's website to see whether they're nursing adorable newborn animals and learn how to muck *in* by volunteering to muck *out*, look after the animals or care for the garden.

1a Goldsmiths Row, E2 8QA
Nearest station: Cambridge Heath
hackneycityfarm.co.uk

18

DALSTON EASTERN CURVE GARDEN

Botanical bliss in Hackney

Sandwiched between two buildings and hidden behind tall wooden gates, you could walk past this garden a hundred times without realising what wonder lies within. Built on the site of the disused Eastern Curve railway line in Hackney, the long and narrow Dalston Curve is filled with plants that bring year-round greenery (all tended by volunteers) and provide a lush community sanctuary in a neighbourhood that would otherwise be a park desert. Stay awhile at the on-site cafe, which serves sweet treats, natural wine, local beers and, in the summer months, wood-fired pizzas. Tables are plentiful, so park yourself with a good book for as long as you like and stay until evening, when you might catch an upbeat live music performance.

13 Dalston Lane, E8 3DF
Nearest station: Dalston Junction
dalstongarden.org

19

LEASIDE TRUST

Paddling paradise in east London

Hackney isn't known as a kayaking destination, and that's why the River Lea is so enticing. On dry land, you'll compete with walkers, runners, cyclists and dogs along the towpaths, but there's rarely traffic on the water. Head to Leaside to join an affordable kayaking session suitable for any skill level, including complete beginners, led by passionate instructors. The charity uses adventure as a force for good, too: in 2025, volunteers kayaked around the canal to clear tonnes of invasive floating pennywort, helping to protect native plants from being choked out. The scenery gets wilder as you paddle north from the Trust's boat launch, so keep an eye out for herons, swans, ducks and even terrapins as you go.

34 Spring Lane, E5 9HQ
Nearest station: Clapton
leaside.org.uk

20

SPRINGFIELD PARK

Hillside haven with views of east London

It's easy to overlook this canalside park if you approach from the towpath alongside the Lee Navigation, which draws runners, walkers and cyclists from all over east London. Its hilltop perch hides its surprising expanse and offers some of the best views over Walthamstow Marshes and the River Lea. Walking paths criss-cross the green and showcase further captivating views of Hackney Marshes and beyond, while hedge-surrounded benches offer shelter from wind and a bit of privacy. Further up the hill, discover woodland trails leading deeper into the park and back down to the canal. Grade II-listed Springfield House and Cafe is a terrific spot for tea, and for a cosy pint, take a short stroll to Clapton's Crooked Billet pub.

Springfield House, E5 9EF
Nearest station: Clapton

21

BECKENHAM PLACE PARK

Massive estate with a plethora of habitats

Once a private estate and later a golf course, this 237-acre south-east London green space has only recently become the destination-worthy park it is today, following a hefty multi-million-pound refurbishment. From the terrace of the Grade II-listed Palladian-style mansion, broad views of the gently rolling grounds and ancient woodland exude *major* country manor vibes. Set off for miles of walking or trail running through the forest; explore its rare wet woodland habitat, bluebell territory and wildflower meadows; or take a dip in the lake – the first in London built specifically for wild swimming. Warm up with a hot drink from one of three on-site cafes, including the Mansion's Bar & Cafe, which serves locally roasted Hundred House Coffee and delights from Blackbird Bakery.

Beckenham Hill Road, BR3 1SY
Nearest station: Beckenham Hill
beckenhamplacepark.com

22
KESTON COMMON

Charles Darwin's research grounds

How many of London's green spaces can claim to have played a vital role in our understanding of evolutionary biology? Tread the trails of Keston Common and you'll follow (quite literally) in the footsteps of Charles Darwin, who often ventured here from his nearby family home to conduct research. The site is composed of heathland, grassland, ponds and a bog where Darwin studied carnivorous plants. Today, visitors fish here for carp, bream and pike (licence required) and watch for herons, kestrels and kingfishers. Download the 'Darwin's Footsteps' trail pamphlet from Bromley Parks for a guide to specific sites that helped shape the naturalist's theories. The route leads all the way to his former home, Down House, where you can visit the greenhouses that played host to his botanical experiments (paid entry).

Fishponds Road, BR2 6HA
Nearest station: Hayes
bromleyparks.co.uk

23

GREENWICH PENINSULA ECOLOGY PARK

Compact nature reserve teeming with wildlife

To say that this beloved urban reserve is a hidden gem is to understate how truly *invisible* it seems if you don't know what you're looking for. The inner boardwalk – mere steps from the busy Thames Path and minutes from the O2 – is enclosed by a tall wooden fence, blocking the view of the tiny, tranquil paradise within. Its central wildflower meadow is alive with insects, and two lakeside bird hides offer stunning marshland views where you can happily sit for an hour to spot snipes, swifts, reed warblers, herons and many other waterfowl species who rest here. There are plenty of ways to get wild on site, from weekly conservation tasks and wildlife walks to guided birdwatching and mudlarking sessions.

John Harrison Way, SE10 0QZ
Nearest station: North Greenwich
tcv.org.uk/greenwichpeninsula

24

CENTRE FOR WILDLIFE GARDENING

Learn how to nurture nature at home

Rewilding your own garden, however small, is a fantastic way to help nature thrive in your community. Get hands-on inspiration at the Centre for Wildlife Gardening, where the London Wildlife Trust (no.5) has transformed a former council depot into a thriving natural habitat. It's easy to imagine how the techniques used here could transform your own patch of green. In the demonstration wildlife garden, a small pond welcomes frogs and toads, weathered wood has been upcycled into bee and bug hotels and a shallow trench filled with logs and bricks offers hideaways for toads and newts. Bring some cash if you're in the market for new flora – a small donation-based plant sale supports the centre while offering affordable greenery to plant at home.

28 Marsden Road, SE15 4EE
Nearest station: East Dulwich
wildlondon.org.uk/nature-reserves/
centre-for-wildlife-gardening

25

AVERY HILL WINTER GARDEN & PARK

Tropical climes in a Victorian glasshouse

No matter the weather outside, the temperature inside the magnificent domed glasshouse at Avery Hill is positively balmy. Operated by the University of Greenwich, this small but perfectly formed Victorian hothouse is open daily, free to visit and houses tropical plants from around the world. Fancy a bit of tree-spotting? Step back out into the fresh air where you'll find paper maps of the mile-long Tree Trail, directing you to 16 significant specimens around the park. Among others, you'll find Black Walnut, English Oaks, London Planes, Scots Pine and Cedar of Lebanon. The Friends of Avery Hill Park group also holds seasonal butterfly and bat monitoring walks to keep track of local species and numbers in the area.

Avery Hill Park, SE9 2PQ
Nearest station: Falconwood
averyhillwintergarden.org.uk

26

GREENWICH PARK

Wild nature amid historic majesty

Known across the globe as the birthplace of Greenwich Mean Time, these 182 acres of diverse habitats – including scrubland, rare acid grassland and woodland – are far more than the sum of their storied history and regal roots. The views of the capital's skyline from the meadowland on One Tree Hill have inspired artists for centuries – just a glimpse is well worth the vertical approach. Downhill, the Queen's Orchard is a tiny walled garden with a delightful air of natural chaos in contrast to the park's manicured lawns. Once a haven for Queen Elizabeth I, here you'll find an orchard of apple, pear and cherry trees. Crops including tomatoes and carrots are planted around a central pond, where reeds, grasses and lavender attract pollinator bees. Retreat here when the garden's gates open during the spring and summer months.

Shooters Hill Road, SE10 8QY
Nearest stations: Greenwich, Maze Hill
royalparks.org.uk

27

OXLEAS WOODLANDS

From cafe to castle through truly ancient woods

Woodlands need only be about 400 years old to classify as 'ancient', but parts of Oxleas date back *thousands* of years – all the way to the last ice age. Formerly part of the grounds of royal residence Eltham Palace, you can now hike freely through stands of oak, silver birch, hornbeam and coppiced hazel so dense, it's hard to see the sky. For a relaxed ramble with purpose, start at Oxleas Wood Cafe and walk about a mile and a half to Severndroog Castle, a Gothic, Grade II-listed, Rapunzel-esque folly with panoramic views from its viewing platform (paid entry; open seasonally on Sundays). The tearoom menu changes weekly, featuring freshly baked pastries and wedges of cake supplied by neighbouring Sitopia Farm.

Crown Woods Lane, SE18 3JA
Nearest station: Falconwood
oxleaswoodlands.uk

28

SYDENHAM HILL WOOD

Birdsong abounds in this rewilded woodland

Nature has recovered well in this wondrous slice of woodland since the Nunhead to Crystal Palace railway line that once passed through here closed more than 70 years ago. Today, all you can hear from the footbridge over the old track are the songs of parakeets and myriad other birds, and the disused tunnel is now a roost for bats. Stick to Cox's Walk and other well-marked paths to give saplings and undergrowth a fighting chance, as heavy footfall has snuffed many sprouts. Keep one eye on the green if you find yourself walking alongside the golf course next door – you may just see a few bold foxes prancing around the holes at dusk. Tack on a visit to the nearby Horniman Museum, which has its own gardens, an excellent cafe, aquarium and tropical Butterfly House.

Crescent Wood Road, SE26 6LS
Nearest station: Sydenham Hill

29

THE TARN

Secret spot for historic walks and birdwatching

If your heart desires an afternoon of reading underneath the curtain of a lakeside weeping willow, look no further: The Tarn may just have the most perfect bench in all of London. Though public now, the site was once part of the grounds of Eltham Palace, and you can still peer down into its 18th-century ice well. Algae blooms sometimes colour the lake bright green in warmer months, which attracts a variety of ducks and geese. The 50-mile Green Chain Walk runs through the park, connecting it to the gardens of the nearby Art Deco palace – about a mile away by trail, less by pavement. If you have time, you won't regret stopping for a cream tea in the cafe's glasshouse.

Court Road, SE9 5AQ
Nearest station: Mottingham
royalgreenwich.gov.uk

30

MORDEN HALL PARK

Thriving wetland

Once a bustling snuff mill, Morden Hall is now a mosaic of diverse habitats ideal for a day of nature exploration. Head to the Wetland Boardwalk for a short but immersive (and buggy-accessible) stroll through reedbeds and bulrushes where you might see herons, snipe and kingfishers. The generous seating area is a perfect post for kids to watch for amphibians while they absorb an illustrated explainer on the life cycle of a frog. Two on-site cafes offer escapes from the elements, as does the Kiln Room, which hosts temporary exhibitions and interactive displays explaining the park's industrial past and the ecosystems you'll find here. Exit via the (first-ever) National Trust Garden Centre, where you might be tempted to rehome some plants on your own grounds.

Morden Hall Road, SM4 5JD
Nearest station: Morden
nationaltrust.org.uk

31

SELSDON WOOD NATURE RESERVE

Cherished woodland, wildflowers and wildlife

It may not get top billing compared with other slices of ancient woodland around London, but Selsdon certainly enjoys rave reviews from its community. This is immediately apparent from a mere glance at the notice boards at the entrance gates listing guided seasonal walks led by the Friends of Selsdon Wood, whose website documents the reserve's history and wildlife in painstaking detail. Peruse the online wildflower gallery before you visit to discover the hundreds of species you can spot here, including the deep-blue alpine speedwell, narcissus, grape hyacinth and even wild strawberries. If the stars align, you may even behold a near-mythical white squirrel.

Old Farleigh Road, CR0 9HW
Nearest station (tram): New Addington
friendsofselsdonwood.co.uk

32

THE WANDLE TRAIL

Industry linchpin turned riverside haven

Once one of the hardest-working rivers in the world, the River Wandle powered dozens of water wheels for snuff and textile mills up and down its banks. Much work has been done to clean it up since then, and today, its shallow waters are crystal-clear along much of the 12.5-mile Wandle Trail. For a moderate 7-mile expedition, start mid-trail at Carshalton Ponds and finish at Morden Hall Park (no.30) to refuel and rest your legs. Along the way, take a full lap of Wilderness Island, a tiny but teeming nature reserve which accommodates woodland, scrub, wetlands and meadows. Cradled by the Croydon and Carshalton branches of the Wandle, its unique combination of habitats draws kingfishers, frogs, Orange-tip butterflies and many other creatures. Wear good boots, as portions of the path can get muddy.

Wandsworth to Croydon
wandle.org/thewandle/thewandletrail

33

WIMBLEDON COMMON

Wildlife, walks and Wombles

With more than a thousand acres to roam, the interconnected Wimbledon and Putney Commons together make up a vast open space. Above ground, there are 16 miles of horse riding trails and below, there are 17 known badger setts. The Commons offer a wealth of habitats for small mammals, including acid grassland, heathland, bogs and woods. While you're unlikely to spot the weasels, moles, voles and shrews that call it home, be sure to pay homage to the fictional eco-conscious *Wombles* by picking up any litter you spot. You can also take a turn around the iconic Wimbledon Windmill. Once every five weeks, rangers release the brakes on the sails (for just half an hour) to make sure everything remains in working order.

Windmill Road, SW19 5NR
Nearest stations: Wimbledon, Southfields
wpcc.org.uk

34

SERPENTINE LIDO

Iconic spot for open water swimming

This legendary swimming lake was originally commissioned by Queen Caroline in the early 18th century to make Hyde Park more scenic. Today, its chlorine-free, unheated waters are open to the public from May to September, and to local ducks, swans, herons and members of the Serpentine Swimming Club year-round. Prospective new members for this historic club (dating back to 1864) are pulled weekly from a waiting list. Still, there is another way to enjoy a bracing winter dip at the Lido if you can't wait: it serves as the third of four frigid plunges in The Swimmer, a hardy half marathon swim/run event hosted by cross-country swimming company Above/Below. Bring a flask of something restoratively hot and book well ahead; the suffering is more enjoyable than you'd predict.

Hyde Park, W2 2UH
Nearest station: Knightsbridge
royalparks.org.uk

35

LONDON WETLAND CENTRE

Spectacular urban habitat

Step through the gates of the London Wetland Centre and you'll feel as though you've been taken on an avian safari. Osprey, Grey Herons, Great White Egrets, Common Cranes, Little Bitterns and a plethora of ducks, teal and geese are just some of the waterfowl you'll spot here from a maze of accessible boardwalks. Once a set of Victorian reservoirs, the site was saved from development in the late '90s and opened in 2000. Today, Sir David Attenborough calls it London's 'extra lung'. Bring your binoculars (or buy some slick new optics in the shop) and get comfortable at any of the six hides. Check the schedule for otter feeding times and when *you* get hungry, the on-site cafe has tea, pastries and hot lunches.

Queen Elizabeth Walk, SW13 9WT
Nearest station: Barnes
wwt.org.uk

36

RICHMOND PARK

Historic landscape with free-roaming deer

It's all too easy to lose track of time and distance in Richmond Park, which is so vast you can find yourself an hour's walk from the nearest road. Ideal for Charles I, who arrived here in 1625 to put distance between himself and the plague-ridden city. Today, the fallow and red deer he brought along for sport still thrive, as do 400,000 ant hills – many pre-dating both World Wars. While much of London has been deforested for centuries, at least one oak here is believed to be 750 years old, and many more at least half that age. Don't miss the woodland gardens of Isabella Plantation and *definitely* don't forget your binoculars – nearly 150 bird species roam the skies including Tawny Owls, kestrels and herons. When it's time for tea, head to the Grade II-listed Pembroke Lodge for scones and spectacular views of the Thames Valley.

Petersham Road, TW10 5HS
Nearest station: Richmond
royalparks.org.uk

37

HORSENDEN HILL

Open-air adventures for all ages

Rain or shine, Horsenden Hill is a stand-out destination for families with restless little ones in need of an outdoor expedition. First things first – fans of the book will love entering the 'deep, dark wood' to take on the Gruffalo Trail, featuring sculptures of characters from the story. Walking on, pass grazing cattle and the tree nursery, where thousands of saplings are being raised to be planted around nearby Ealing. Aspiring ornithologists and wildlife biologists should take note of the impressive Seasonal Wildlife information board, which highlights the kestrels, goldfinches, frogs and shrews you might encounter, and when you're likely to spot them. The adjacent Horsenden Farm sells treats for all ages: baked goods, ice cream and caffeine fixes from Horsenden Loaf microbakery and beers from Perivale Brewery.

Horsenden Lane North, UB6 7PQ
Nearest station: Perivale
horsenden.org

38

TERRACE GARDENS

A view so scenic, it's protected by Parliament

Start your visit at the top of Richmond Hill to discover why the breathtaking view from Terrace Gardens is protected by an Act of Parliament – the only English landscape to enjoy such a privilege. From here, you'll see the curve of the Thames as it wraps around Marble Hill. Beautiful at any time of day, the riverscape is especially entrancing in the early morning light, when mist and fog roll over the grasses below. As well as its ancient trees and manicured borders, the park offers prime habitats for local wildlife, with insect-friendly plants and a woodland garden featuring stag beetle loggeries and bee homes. Pause for hot drinks, pastries and vegetarian lunches at the Hollyhock or its sister cafe, the riverside Tide Tables, before embarking on your (rather steep) walk back up the hill.

Petersham Road, TW10 6RH
Nearest station: Richmond
richmond.gov.uk

39

NEW RIVER PATH

Picturesque route along a 17th-century aqueduct

Back in 1613, the New River was just that: a sparkling aqueduct built to bring fresh water from Hertfordshire to the capital. Incredibly, it still provides about eight per cent of the city's water, though very little of the channel remains in its original form. The way-marked trail starts at the south bank of the River Lea and ends at Rosebery Avenue in the heart of Islington, passing by repurposed historic waterworks. Don't miss The Castle, a fortress-like former pumping station that's now a climbing centre, and adjacent nature reserve Woodberry Wetlands (no.45). With good transport links and plentiful pubs and cafes along the way, it would be an enjoyable endeavour to tackle the whole 28-mile trail over a long weekend. End your journey at Pophams bakery to indulge in an unparalleled cardamom bun.

Hertford to Islington

40

WELSH HARP
OPEN SPACE

Exhilarating watersports surrounded by woodland

A renowned destination for Londoners since Victorian times, Welsh Harp Open Space was once so popular it had its own rail station, serving day-trippers seeking clean air and good times. It's far more serene today, but its adventurous spirit lives on – take a windsurfing lesson, join one of several sailing clubs or rent kayaks or canoes waterside for a leisurely paddle. Even on a cold, rainy winter day, you're likely to see people out on the water. If you'd rather keep your land legs, take a peaceful stroll on the woodland paths that crisscross along the water's edge, keeping an eye out for colourful Orange-tip and Peacock butterflies, and enjoy a welcome dose of wilderness.

Birchen Grove, NW9 7LY
Nearest station: Hendon
brent.gov.uk

41

WALTHAMSTOW WETLANDS

Wildlife-abundant reservoirs and fishery

The ten reservoirs here were engineering feats when they were dug in the 1800s, mostly by hand. Today, the site provides water for 3.5 million Londoners as well as being a remarkable reserve for birds of prey; a destination for trout, bream and perch fishing (licence required); and an enriching, kid-friendly day out in nature. Take your binoculars on a wander or settle into one of two hides to watch for kingfishers, Grey Herons and Peregrine falcons. At ground level, keep your eyes peeled for snuffling European hedgehogs. Learn about the site's industrial past at the visitor centre, allowing time for a cup of locally roasted Liberty Coffee at the Engine House Cafe. Be sure to check out seasonal events, including guided nature walks, stargazing and insect DNA mapping.

2 Forest Road, N17 9NH
Nearest stations: Tottenham Hale, Blackhorse Road
wildlondon.org.uk /nature-reserves/
walthamstow-wetlands

42

WEST RESERVOIR

Vast wild swimming reservoir

In the heart of Hackney, West Reservoir is one of two adjacent freshwater sites built by the New River Company in the early 19th century, using stones salvaged from the demolition of the medieval London Bridge to line the banks. Saved from development in the '90s, today, the 23-acre reservoir is one of the city's largest and most exhilarating destinations for swimming, paddling and sailing, as well as being a haven for local wildlife. Book ahead for an open-water swim session, available year-round (wetsuits recommended during the icy winter months), or arrive unannounced to unwind in the cafe with waterside views. For an adrenaline rush, take a sailing lesson or join Castle Canoe Club, where you can try canoe polo or a relaxed paddle on Sunday mornings.

Green Lanes, N4 2HA
Nearest station: Manor House
hackney.gov.uk

43

GROVELANDS PARK

Tranquil park nestled in suburbia

Step inside this green space, surrounded by suburban homes and leafy streets, and the sights and sounds of the city will fade in an instant. Grade II-listed Grovelands was a private estate for centuries before it became a park in 1913. Its intriguing trivia includes tales of 'The Witch of Edmonton', who lived in dense woodland nearby, and a population of wild terrapins – discarded pets from the *Teenage Mutant Ninja Turtles* mania in the '90s. Today, magic can be found in the natural play area tucked into the woods, and by enjoying a peaceful picnic on the grassy hills or talking a serene stroll around the lake. Peckish? The park's cafe serves light refreshments for both people and birds. Pick up a snack for yourself and a bag of seeds to feed the waterfowl around the lake.

The Bourne, N14 6RA
Nearest station: Southgate
friendsofgrovelands.co.uk

44

HAMPSTEAD HEATH

Sweeping scenery, stargazing and swimming

The rugged hills of Hampstead Heath seem to exist in an alternate universe, where life feels deliciously rural and slow-paced. It gets dark enough here to gaze at shooting stars during meteor showers and mobile phone signal is sketchy at best, adding to the feeling of being in the countryside. Its three swimming ponds – the Men's, Ladies' and Mixed – were originally dug as reservoirs in the 17th and 18th centuries and are a hot spot for Londoners, ducks and herons – even when icy-cold. You won't find much luxury in the changing rooms, where warm showers are in short supply, but an invigorating dip is always worth the chill. Take care if you bring refreshments with you (Highgate Village has no shortage of cafes), as resident foxes are skilled at stealing sandwiches from rucksacks.

Hampstead Heath, NW3 1BP
Nearest station: Hampstead Heath
cityoflondon.gov.uk

45

WOODBERRY
WETLANDS

Young nature reserve and bird habitat

From a Victorian drinking-water reservoir for a wealthy neighbourhood to a grim post-war housing estate – and then back again to relative glitz – Woodberry Wetlands has been on quite a journey. It was only recently spared from the hands of developers, when it was opened by Sir David Attenborough as a nature reserve in 2016. Since then, it has been spoiled for biodiversity. Here, you may spot Arctic Terns, the neon-bright green-and-yellow Siskin, kestrels, kingfishers, Northern Lapwings and dozens of other native and migrating birds. Take an easy loop around the reservoir, making a pit stop for refreshments at the Coal House Cafe's rooftop patio, before continuing on to the adjacent West Reservoir (no.42) for a bracing wild swim.

New River Path, Lordship Road, N16 5HQ
Nearest stations: Manor House, Stamford Hill
wildlondon.org.uk/nature-reserves/woodberry-wetlands

46

REGENT'S PARK & CANAL

Grand green space where nature thrives

Few urban paddling trails can compete with the Regent's Canal, which is both exhilarating and serene. Though busy elsewhere, the canal is calm, verdant and enchanting where it passes through Regent's Park, overlooked by London Zoo's lofty aviary. On foot, take the Broad Walk for a tree-lined stroll out of sight of city roads and don't miss Queen Mary's Rose Gardens, where you'll lose count of how many different varieties adorn the grounds (spoiler: there are more than 12,000 roses across 85 varieties). With woodland, grass-land and wetland, the park is a rich habitat for city critters, including one of London's last breed-ing populations of hedgehogs. Early birds should hustle to Primrose Hill before daybreak to witness a spectacular sunrise over the capital.

Chester Road, NW1 4NR
Nearest stations: Regent's Park, Baker Street
royalparks.org.uk

47

ABNEY PARK CEMETERY

Burial ground where nature reigns supreme

When it was founded in 1840 as Europe's first fully non-denominational cemetery, this Grade II-listed park – one of London's 'Magnificent Seven' garden cemeteries – was a well-manicured arboretum. In the '70s, it fell into disrepair, allowing its trees, grasses and ivy to grow as they pleased, overtaking every inch of the grounds. In 1993, it became Hackney's first nature reserve and today, its nettles, crocuses, bluebells and grasses attract bees and butterflies aplenty. Pop by the new cafe at the entrance, then get lost amid the rows of historic headstones and overgrown graves that have been jumbled by determined tree roots. Join a guided tour if you'd rather not roam alone.

219 Stoke Newington High Street, N16 0LH
Nearest station: Stoke Newington
abneypark.org

48

BENTLEY PRIORY NATURE RESERVE

Trails, trees and a (very) mighty oak

Pass through a narrow pathway to gain entry into this historic green space and the hum of the city will soon be a distant memory. Bentley Priory was first mentioned in the Domesday Book in 1086 and today, its grounds remain undeveloped and serene. Follow the circular walk and use the QR codes on signposts (or the guides on their website) to read about its plant species, site history and wildlife, including the resident herd of fallow deer. If you do nothing else, be sure to visit 'The Master', a storied ancient oak tree believed to be almost 500 years old (you can find it pinned on Google Maps). Lace up your boots (it can get muddy) and be prepared to run into grazing cattle along the way.

Stanmore, HA7 3LY
Nearest station: Stanmore
harrowncf.org

49
THE PARKLAND WALK

Hidden woodland trail through north London

It's easy to miss the 5 km Parkland Walk, and that's the best thing about it – it's largely contained within a green corridor that feels protected from city chaos. The tree-canopied path follows an old railway line from Finsbury Park through the ancient Queen's Wood (no.50), ending at Alexandra Palace. In spring, the section around Crouch End is fantastic for foraging wild garlic and bluebells carpet bits of woodland around the trail. Bring your binoculars to watch for kestrels, finches, tits, woodpeckers and about 60 species of butterfly. The walk is gorgeous year-round, but it's at its best – and busiest – in warmer months, when deciduous trees block views of the roads.

Finsbury Park to Alexandra Palace
Nearest stations: Finsbury Park, Alexandra Palace
parkland-walk.org.uk

50

QUEEN'S WOOD

Stunning woodland with fairy-tale cafe

Lock eyes on Queen's Wood Cafe, engulfed by oak, beech and hornbeam trees, and you'd be forgiven for thinking you'd slipped into a Grimm's fairy-tale dreamscape. Nestled within Queen's Wood's 52 acres, this 19th-century former wood-keeper's lodge has turned the surrounding forest into a bucket list destination. More than just a place to stop for tea, this vibrant hub offers food-growing and composting workshops, exhibits work from local artists and hosts nature-based therapy sessions in a serene eco-cabin. Start at the cafe for a loop through the wood, listening for woodpeckers as you wander. Delight in carpets of bluebells in spring and spot snowdrops in winter. Much of the organic produce grown in the cafe's award-winning, volunteer-run garden ends up on the menu in fresh sandwiches and salads.

Queen's Wood Road, N6 6UU
Nearest station: Highgate
haringey.gov.uk

51
HIGHGATE WOOD

Thriving biodiversity in untamed woodland

Just across the street from Queen's Wood (no.50), Highgate Wood is a dreamy place for a stroll alongside gnarled oaks and twisted hornbeams. Biodiversity is meticulously tracked here: you'll find over 350 species of fungi, 70 species of bird (including the majestic Tawny Owl) and seven species of bats, which hunt at dusk for over 400 species of moth. Thanks to a no-cycling policy, the paths are peaceful for pedestrians, joggers and free, volunteer-guided nature walks focusing on tree and fungi identification. At the centre of the wood, you'll find a wildlife information hut and the Pavilion Cafe, run by London-based falafel makers, Hoxton Beach. In spring, wander between Bridge Gate and Cranley Gate, past the site of an ancient Roman pottery kiln, for the best chance of spotting waves of bluebells amid the trees.

Muswell Hill Road, N10 3JN
Nearest station: Highgate
cityoflondon.gov.uk

52

STANMORE COUNTRY PARK

Rewilded farm with incredible views of London

Ride the Tube north to Stanmore, the very end of the Jubilee line, and walk for just a few short minutes. As you step into the dense woodland of Stanmore Country Park, you'll instantly forget you're in the city. Follow trail markers leading to the 'London Viewpoint', where you'll be greeted by one of the grandest hilltop views the capital has to offer – on a clear day, you'll easily spot Wembley stadium, the London Eye and The Shard. Covering 76 acres, this park and nature reserve is home to a multitude of flora and fauna, including muntjac deer. Visit in spring when the woodland is blanketed by bluebells and, if you enjoy foraging, bring a container with you in August, when blackberry brambles laden with plump fruit line the trails.

Kerry Avenue, HA7 4NN
Nearest station: Stanmore
harrowncf.org

53

TRENT COUNTRY PARK

Trek, ride or zip line across acres of parkland

Like many of London's most majestic green spaces, Trent Country Park was once private land reserved for royal hunting pursuits, known as Enfield Chase. Today, this 413-acre public park provides recreational diversions for all stripes, with miles of gentle forest walks, a sublimely serene Japanese water garden and the Wildlife Rescue and Ambulance Service Animal Centre, where you can meet resident sheep, ponies, goats and deer – not forgetting Terry the terrapin. To run down the kids' batteries (or your own), sign up for a horse riding lesson from Trent Park Equestrian Centre or clip in for Go Ape's Treetop Challenge, a high ropes course that will send you whizzing through the woods on zip lines up to 125 metres long.

Cockfosters Road, EN4 0JY
Nearest station: Cockfosters
trentcountrypark.com

54

DARLANDS NATURE RESERVE

Glorious Green Belt walks

Once you've hopped off the Northern line at Totteridge, trekking to Darlands might feel like a bit of a quest. It's well worth the walk. Surrounded by other green spaces, and lovingly tended by local volunteers, this protected woodland feels truly unspoiled. Tuck away your phone for a lap around the lake, zig-zagging Folly Brook along the way, and marvel at the carpets of moss crawling up trailside tree trunks. View violets in spring, snowdrops in winter and (if you're lucky) you might even spot the elusive Dunnock, a shy bird that hides among the undergrowth. Stick to the paths to protect both the environment and yourself – in summer, invasive and poisonous Giant Hogweed can grow unruly, and its sap can burn your skin if you touch it.

Totteridge Village, N20 8PJ
Nearest stations: Totteridge & Whetstone, Woodside Park
darlandsconservationtrust.org

55

TITSEY PLACE
& GARDENS

Breathtaking views of the North Downs

Driving up to the car park for one of Titsey's woodland walks is an adventure in itself; with such a twisty, narrow road, it feels like driving straight up a mountain. Once you reach the trails, however, your blood pressure will instantly recede. Though steep in places, Titsey's forested foot-paths and bridleway offer sweeping, bucolic views of picture-perfect green and pleasant land. Plan your outing between May and September, when the historic manor house and gardens are open for (paid) visits. Stroll through the glasshouses, rose beds and walled Victorian kitchen garden, then indulge in a delectable afternoon tea in the estate's Tea Room.

Pitchfont Lodge, Water Lane, RH8 0SA
Nearest station: Oxted
titsey.org

56

WAKEHURST

Kew's wild botanic garden in Sussex

Explore 535 astounding acres of diverse landscapes at Wakehurst, the lesser-known sister of Kew Gardens. Here, in a 'living laboratory' of flora and fauna, you can roam woods, wetlands and gardens emulating habitats from Asia, the Americas and beyond – from a ramble across its American prairie to a fragrant wander through the woodlands of Australia, surrounded by the scents of pine and eucalyptus. This vast botanic garden is also home to a plethora of wild animal species including the protected dormouse, barn owls and grass snakes, with special trails allowing for sightings. Citizen scientists of all ages should visit the Millennium Seed Bank Atrium, offering an insight into its collection of 40,000 plant species hailing from across the globe, making it the most biodiverse place on the planet.

Ardingley, Haywards Heath, RH17 6TN
Nearest station: Haywards Heath
kew.org/wakehurst

57

CHESS VALLEY WALK

From the Tube to the Chilterns

The Chilterns Area of Outstanding Natural Beauty does precisely what it says on the tin: it's baffling that views this jaw-dropping can be witnessed mere steps from the Metropolitan line. Hop off the Tube at either Chesham or Rickmansworth and spend the day trekking ten stunning miles along the Chess Valley Walk, which follows the eponymous crystal-clear chalk stream stretching between the two stations. The trail is well marked, but the picturesque scenery can easily distract you from your sense of direction, so take care to check signposts at intersections with other footpaths. Watch for water voles, the iridescent blue–green Demoiselle damselfly and Little Egrets wading in the river. If you've worked up a thirst from your fresh-air pursuits, there are ample options for a satisfying pint to round off your journey.

Chesham to Rickmansworth
Nearest stations: Chesham, Rickmansworth
chilterns.org.uk/map_marker/chess-valley-walk

58

FIR & POND WOODS

Trail through idyllic farmland and forest

Just beyond the M25 – and well within earshot –
Fir & Pond Woods may not, at first glance, appear
to be the most peaceful place for wildlife. But
somehow, despite the incessant thrum of traffic,
nature thrives in this small patch of ancient woodland, where the undergrowth is dense with ferns.
Listen for woodpeckers and keep an eye out for
Shetland sheep in the meadows, which the Herts
& Middlesex Wildlife Trust employ as their 'living
lawnmowers'. Be sure to wear your wellies and
consider bringing walking sticks if you go after
rainfall, as the uneven paths can get muddy and
slick. Bring a flask of tea or coffee with you, too,
as you'll be miles from anyone selling it.

Coopers Lane Road, EN6 4DG
Nearest station: Potters Bar
hertswildlifetrust.org.uk

59

AMWELL NATURE RESERVE

Birdwatching heaven

Once a gravel pit, Amwell Nature Reserve today is a scenic, thriving habitat for a wide variety of winged visitors. You'll hear them before you see them; the rare and elusive resident Bittern is the UK's loudest bird, with a mating call that booms through the reeds for a 3-mile radius. You'll find identification guides posted around the reserve, including in the White Hide – always open – with fantastic views of Great Hardmead Lake. There, you might see kites, herons, terns, egrets, owls and myriad ducks, geese and gulls. Reach the reserve by walking south from Ware or north from St Margarets along the Lee Navigation towpath, a picturesque route lined with vintage narrowboats.

Amwell Lane, SG12 9SS
Nearest station: St Margarets
hertswildlifetrust.org.uk

60
SEVEN SISTERS WALK

Dramatic hike atop white chalk cliffs

The Seven Sisters are one of the most majestic sights in England, and these dramatic chalk cliffs are splayed in front of you for the whole of this 13-mile coastal walk. Start at Seaford Beach and follow the trail all the way to Eastbourne, where you can celebrate your hike with an ice cream on the Pier. On a sunny day, the gleaming cliffs glisten against the sea and it may be hard to resist a wild swim at Birling Gap – a welcome break at the halfway point of your adventure. Allow yourself plenty of time and study the bus route in advance so you don't miss a ride back to town if your legs beg for a rest.

Seaford Beach to Eastbourne
Nearest stations: Seaford, Eastbourne
sevensisters.org.uk

61

UNPLUGGED

An untethered weekend of off-grid adventure

Forget airplane mode. When you check into an Unplugged cabin, you'll quarantine your phone all weekend and trade your screens for their analogue ancestors: a cassette player, an Instax camera, board games, a Nokia dumbphone, a map and compass, and a bunch of actual books. At first, the hours may drag as you stoke the fire of your off-grid abode and stare out of the windows into peaceful farmland or forest views. But soon, as the digital detox takes hold, you'll never want to go online again. There are dozens of cabins to choose from, dotted around England and Wales – many within just an hour's drive of London. All are designed to feel peaceful and secluded. So, turn off the tech, tune in to the sights, sounds and smells of nature, and don't forget to look up – beyond the inextinguishable city lights, the stars are stunning.

Various locations
unplugged.rest

62
ARCHITECT'S HOLIDAY

Artful cabins hidden deep within woodland

The ultra-chic cabins at Architect's Holiday stop just short of merging fully with nature. In their original wooden (and off-grid) Cabin X, floor-to-ceiling windows in the bathroom lend the feeling of showering among the lush, green ferns. Each cabin has been painstakingly built with reclaimed, recycled and sustainable materials and has its own personality – such as the brand-new Bather's cabin, a splurge-worthy retreat with private sauna, secret rooftop hot tub and plunge pool. A session in the iconic red sauna (right), with its gigantic, forest-facing window, is an absolute must. At night, listen for the hoots of owls and watch for deer rustling in the bushes. Whatever you do, don't leave the on-site farm shop and cafe without nabbing a batch of their giant scones – heaven.

Great Park Farm, TN33 9DT
Nearest station: Battle
architects.holiday

63

HOGSMILL RIVER WALK

Waterside views inspiring artists for centuries

It was along the banks of the Hogsmill that artist John Everett Millais painted *Ophelia*, and this chalk stream, supporting an abundance of plant life, is no less inspiring today. Follow the riverside trail seven miles from Ewell to Kingston for a peaceful, tree-canopied walk through a series of underrated green spaces, including Chamber Mead Wetlands, created in 2024 to filter out pollution. Get set for a wealth of wildlife-watching, as the spot makes an attractive new home for nesting kingfishers and Little Egrets, not to mention eels, trout and water voles. When the river brings you to Ewell Court Park, take a pleasant detour to meander alongside the pond, with its bird haven called Duck Island, and settle in for lunch at The Secret Garden, on the grounds of Ewell Court House.

Ewell to Kingston
Nearest stations: Ewell, Kingston

64

RIVER LEE COUNTRY PARK

Fresh-air adventures with room to roam

Just west of the more famous Epping Forest (no.10), this 1,000-acre park truly has it all. Stretch your legs on woodland walks, cycle paths up to 20 km long and test your orienteering skills on trails you'll need a map and compass to navigate. Explore the ancient ruins of the Waltham Abbey Gardens, then take a walk in the tranquil Cornmill Meadows nearby. Keep an eye out for dragon-flies – there are so many species in the meadows, it's protected as a dragonfly sanctuary. Kids and grown-ups alike will learn something new at the stunning Wildlife Discovery Centre, which has a spacious hide to spy on birds and a tower to climb for views of the park. You may need to stay over-night at one of the park's 'almost wild' campsites (open seasonally) to do it all.

Waltham Abbey to Broxbourne
Nearest stations: Cheshunt, Waltham Cross, Broxbourne
visitleevalley.org.uk/river-lee-country-park

IMAGE CREDITS

For the foxes, who have always brought me good luck.
With thanks to the Society of Authors for all their support.

An Opinionated Guide to Wild London
First edition, first printing

Published in 2026 by Hoxton Mini Press, London.
Copyright © Hoxton Mini Press 2026. All rights reserved.

Text by Kassondra Cloos
Editing by Kate Overy
Production design by Dom Grant
Production control by David Brimble
Proofreading by Florence Ward
Editorial support by Richard Enright

With thanks to Matthew Young for
initial series design.

Please note: we recommend checking the
websites listed for each entry before you
visit for the latest information on price,
opening times and pre-booking
requirements.

A CIP catalogue record for this book is
available from the British Library.

ISBN: 978-1-917719-16-2

Printed and bound by OZGraf, Poland

Manufacturer: Hoxton Mini Press, 104
Northside Studios, 16–29 Andrews Road,
London E8 4QF, UK
www.hoxtonminipress.com

Represented by: Authorised Rep
Compliance Ltd., Ground Floor, 71 Lower
Baggot Street, Dublin D02 P593, Ireland
www.arccompliance.com

Hoxton Mini Press is an environmen-
tally conscious publisher, committed
to offsetting our carbon footprint.
This book is 100 per cent carbon
compensated, with offset purchased
from Stand For Trees.

Every time you order from our website, we
plant a tree: www.hoxtonminipress.com

Selected opinionated guides in the series:

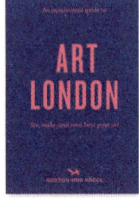

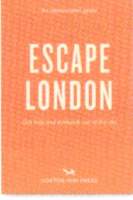

For more go to www.hoxtonminipress.com

INDEX